A   P R A C T I

TRANSRACIAL ADOPTION

WRITTEN BY ISAAC ETTER

Identity

equipping parents empowering children

Table of Contents

INTRODUCTION

"Should I let my Black teenage son say the N-word?"

This question was posed to me by a white adoptive mom during a training I led on zoom in 2020. It was evident from the chat box that she was not the only person with this question. As a white adoptive parent, you are probably already trying to navigate hard conversations with friends, family, and children about race. How do you know the right answer to a question like that? You probably want to know my response. I said, "No, you shouldn't let your Black teenager say the N word".

A Black child in a white home and most likely white community saying the N-word will most likely lead to uncomfortable and complicated experiences and conversations they won't know how to navigate. Once they are an adult, they can make their own choices about language, but your role is to protect them from dangerous and or harmful experiences which they will have if they are casually saying the N word in white environments.

But this is just one of many complex questions I've been asked over the past four years. Over this time, I have gotten the honor of leading training on transracial adoption for many adoptive and foster parents. After years of getting many of the same questions, one thing became apparent to me. Parents that intentionally pursued learning about the complexities of transracial adoption understood they needed a different set of tools to parent their transracial children than their same-race children. However, they were still confused about the exact steps and conversations they should be having with their transracial and biological children about race, culture, and adoption. This book will answer those questions.

You understand race is important and racial Identity is important - I want to help you put it into action at each stage of your child's development so they grow up feeling seen and valued for all the aspects of their identity.

MY STORY

*I*n mid-September of 2018, I walked into an adoption agency office to speak at one of their Cultural Trainings. This was only the second time I would be telling my story in front of an audience, the first being an event I hosted about adoption a month prior. As I was being introduced, sweat started to run down my back and I was panicking, wondering why in the world I thought it would be a good idea to start sharing my story. But as I started to talk, I remember noticing the class's attention focus on my words, hearing gasps at certain parts of my story, and seeing smiles at others.

For the first time, I was sharing hard moments: The rejection I felt from my family and community when I started talking about racism in America in 2016. Having people I knew and loved respond with "When did you become black?" Classmates in college asking, "None of this affects you, so why do you care?" It wasn't the ignorance of their comments that bothered me. It was the complete disregard for my experience as a Black man in America and as a Black person in general. A disregard that I've felt my whole life from people thinking they can call me "nigga" or say it in front of me because "my family was white and I was basically one of them" or being told that I "talk white." This was a blatant and constant disregard for my Blackness as if by being adopted I no longer held the weight or the honor of being a Black person.

But I also shared beautiful moments, moments that came in the midst of thinking that if I continued to speak out about racial injustice, it would cost me my family. Like my parents sharing what they learned from the Malcolm X biography and later defending my work in front of their peers. Like my younger sister becoming a voice in her friend group about injustice and giving a speech on Malcolm X at a Christian debate tournament, even though she knew that it would be an unpopular topic with the conservative community. It was in these moments I started to understand the impact I had on my family.

I also remember sharing heavy memories of adoption that I had never talked about out loud, such as my relationship with my birth mother as a kid and our relationship now. For the first time, I shared that while I was growing up, my birth mother would reach out to my mom to send me stuff for my birthday… but nothing would ever come. I shared how when I was working at a summer camp out of state, my mom called me on my 18th birthday to ask if it was okay to give my birth mother my address so she could send me something for my birthday. I waited all summer but nothing ever came.

I felt that heartbreak all over again in front of these strangers. I left that afternoon feeling emotionally drained and exhausted, realizing for the first time that I had put all of myself out there. I put a vulnerable and fragile search for identity and acceptance into the open in front of families considering adopting. I felt exposed, and yet I went back the next month to do it again. This time the Q&A segment got longer. I was fielding questions about my own identity search and questions like, "Why do Black people have issues with the police?" or "If I raise my Black child on a farm will they feel Black enough?" I had opened the doors for white people to ask the questions they had always wanted to ask but knew they shouldn't ask out loud. This was a delicate position for me to fall into and I knew that if I was going to continue, I had to find a balance that would respect my boundaries, but also accomplish the work I wanted to do. I started focusing my speaking on how we talk about racial issues and how to work through our own bias, using my personal story. After that second talk, I never looked back.

Helping families wrestle with hard questions around race and identity became my passion. I went from speaking once per month to speaking multiple times a month, eventually opening a business to help families who were adopting transracially. Sharing my story has become a joy, but an adoption story is a hard thing, it is full of confusion and pain. It is not a journey that has an end; it is a journey of always learning more about yourself and your broken history. Even though my talks often end with closure, there is a lot that can upset that closure. There are so many unanswered questions that come with being an adoptee. But the question that people keep asking is, "How did you get *here?*"

On June 11, 1998, a teenager in Orange County, New Jersey gave birth to me, Keshaun Malik. For two years, we moved from place to place eventually landing in Fredericksburg, Virginia. There, my birth mother decided adoption was the smartest thing to do with me because of her circumstances. At the age of two, I was brought to an adoption agency and on that same day, Bruce and Julie Etter went to that same agency in search of a child. In the next year, I was adopted by Bruce and Julie, and my name was changed to Isaac Etter.

For a few years after being adopted we lived in Virginia, and I saw my birth mother quite often since the adoption was open. My adoptive parents tell stories of picking her up from work and us all being very involved in each other's lives. I do not have many memories of my birth mother, except one. One of the last times I saw her was at Chuck E Cheese. She and her boyfriend had come with us, and I remember being in the parking lot and saying goodbye to her and her boyfriend. Then: nothing. Apparently, there was one other time I saw her at a McDonald's to say goodbye. She and her boyfriend were moving to Las Vegas. But I don't remember that time. Maybe my mind shut it out, maybe I just simply don't remember, but that was the last time I saw my birth mother. I was four.

A year later we moved into a home my parents bought in Lancaster, Pennsylvania so my dad could work at a school in the area. The small Christian school I went to was one of the first places where I noticed I looked different than everyone else. I remember the one Black family whose children also attended this school. Their son was quite a few years older than me. At one point when I was in first grade, he gave me a durag. Neither my parents nor I knew what to do with it, but this memory has always stuck in my head. They were the only people I knew who looked like me for a few years. My parents ended up homeschooling me starting in 3rd grade due to my academic struggles. It wasn't until a year or two into being homeschooled, that my mother found some homeschool groups and I made some friends who were also adopted and Black. Going into middle school, my best friends were these adopted friends I met through homeschool co-op. By this time, my dad had started working for an online classical Christian school and all my siblings were now being homeschooled as well. My identity issues progressed with me as I headed into teenage activities like church youth group. I was one of three Black children in the youth group and all of us were adopted. This was one of the only settings where I wasn't the only Black person.

But even with other Black people around, the desire to look like everyone else and "fit in" was what I really wanted. I distinctly remember coming home from youth group, running up the stairs to get ready for bed, walking in the bathroom, looking in the mirror, and being disappointed, because I saw a Black boy in the mirror. I wanted to look like everyone around me, I wanted to be white. While I never knew a time I actually *hated* being Black, I also never remember a time I *liked* being Black.

As I headed into high school I also became less conscious of my skin tone. Even though all of my best friends at this point were white, being Black became mostly an afterthought. I would only be self-conscious about it when I wasn't good at sports because people would say I should be because I am black, or when someone pointed out that I wouldn't fit any of the characters in our high school theater musicals. My social life changed dramatically; I made new friends and we did everything together. All of us were in the same homeschool group and choir, so once a week we all went to class together and we often got together on other days and nights. We all were involved in theater and musicals as well. I started doing lighting and sound for these shows towards the end of middle school while all of my friends would act in them.

But I never thought about racism or really knew what racism was growing up. I never remember being treated differently than my white friends or thinking they thought of me as different from them. The summer before my senior year, I turned sixteen. That summer, one of the most popular online platforms was Tumblr. I started a Tumblr and used it to look up F. Scott Fitzgerald quotes, browse through funny videos and pictures, and share with my friends who also used Tumblr. One day I came across a hashtag on Tumblr, #blackoutday. Curious, I clicked on it to find Black people across the country posting pictures in all-black outfits to protest racial injustice. As a sixteen-year-old, I had never seen these kinds of posts or heard about racial injustice. Diving deeper, I learned about a rising movement called Black Lives Matter. Police killing Black people? Racism? These stories, videos, and pictures stuck with me and broke my heart. I was a confused teenager with white parents, learning about a very different side of the culture I grew up in.

Racism? I didn't think that existed, but if it did, why hadn't it happened to me? Had it happened to me and I didn't know? Was my family racist? How could they be racist—I'm Black! My mind raced this entire year with endless questions and observations. I watched how my family, friends, and community talked about Obama as president. I noticed subtle things I hadn't before, like how in almost all the musicals I did, I was cast as a slave or servant boy. I saw how my mother was scared for me to get my driver's license, even though we had never talked about police violence. So many doubts sounded in my head about race. I still wasn't sure if racism was real, but I also couldn't deny the videos and articles I was watching and reading online. I didn't have any Black friends that weren't also adopted, which made it harder. I didn't have anyone to talk to. It was just me in my room, confused, scared, and alone.

Everything was changing with this new exposure to Black culture and struggles. The first time I saw a Black woman that I was attracted to was on Tumblr. I never thought Black women were attractive growing up, but I also only knew one. I realized that I was never shown any beauty in my Blackness; no one talked about it, so I certainly didn't. The guys the girls liked growing up were white. The few Black guys were not fought over. My taste in music was also affected. I started listening to artists like Childish Gambino, as his music often expressed the same identity struggles I was experiencing. His verses often talked about him being called white which I could relate to. When he said, "The only white rapper who's allowed to say the n-word" or "What is this nigga doin rap is for real blacks", these lyrics would hit me hard. I did not know the first thing about being Black, but I did know what it was like to be referred to as a white person constantly despite my skin tone. I would play these songs on loop. In a time when I did not have anyone to go to, these songs made me feel like I was not alone. I also got curious about different Black hairstyles. For the first time, I found a local barber shop. The first time I went in, I waited for about forty minutes because I assumed you just waited for your turn like the shops my parents would take me to when I was growing up. Eventually, someone asked me if I was waiting for a haircut. They made fun of me and told me I need to speak up next time I come into the shop. That was one of my first interactions with a Black man and I remember feeling nervous and embarrassed the whole time. I kept wondering if they knew I wasn't raised by Black parents. I left like a complete outsider. I ended up growing out my hair into an afro, even having it turned into dreads twice. I looked ridiculous, but I was trying to figure this whole Black thing out. There was no tour guide for me on this journey of cultural expression. It was just me and Tumblr trying to figure it out.

When I had a question about Black culture or wanted to understand something, I would run to the Black power pages and read for hours. There was a huge conflict inside of me though. I was trying to balance what I was reading on the internet with the world I was raised in. Was I supposed to believe my parents are racist because they didn't have Black friends? Or because they voted Republican? Was I racist since I held their beliefs? Was any of what I was reading online the truth? I spent my senior year of high school secretly wrestling with these questions. I didn't love my family or friends any less, but none of them knew what I was learning about when I wasn't with them.

My senior year went by in a flash. Graduation was a beautiful time as well. The ceremony was like a regular graduation ceremony, but our parents would come up and hand us our diplomas. I was the only Black person in that 2015 graduating class.

My birthday fell about two weeks after graduation on June 11th. I threw a small party with a few close friends. Afterward, my two best friends spent the night. My friends enjoyed going on long walks at night during the summer and this night we went out after midnight, and they were being extra loud. After walking around the neighborhoods near my house, we decided to head back to my house where we were staying. As we were walking down a long hill, a cop car at the top of the hill started flashing a spotlight around as if it were looking for someone. Immediately we all ran as fast as we could, assuming someone made a noise complaint. In the heat of running, one of my friends says, "It's alright! Isaac is the only one that's gonna get in trouble."

That, right there. It all clicked at once. All the videos, articles, protesting, and rage I had seen online instantly made sense to me. I was in my room on Tumblr, questioning whether racism was real, while my friends knew. They knew they would be fine no matter what happened. They knew I would be treated differently. They knew I was worth less than a white person.

RACIAL IDENTITY DEVELOPMENT FOR ADOPTEES

*M*y racial identity journey started after my 17th birthday. Over the coming years, I would drop out of my all-white Bible college and move to Georgia to just be around Black people and start a new life. My parents would take time to learn about race and racism, something I'm extremely grateful they pursued on their own when they saw the pain I was experiencing.

In Georgia, I spent a lot of time in Atlanta at Morehouse College, a historically Black college. It was there that I started to be able to see myself as a Black person. I grew up seeing almost nobody that was Black so my only reference for how Black people were was what I heard and saw on TV and in the media. When I got to Atlanta, I was confronted with a completely different reality than I expected. I met Black people who had two doctors as parents and talked exactly like me, Black people from middle-class lives, Black people from low-income environments, and everything in between. My assumptions about being Black shattered with each day. By the end of my time in Atlanta, I realized that no matter my experience as an adoptee, I was a Black person and would always be seen as a Black person regardless of where or how I grew up by the world. Though a scary reality, it also freed me up to not feel so self-conscious around people that looked exactly like me. I got lucky, though. I was young and many adoptees don't have the opportunity to just drop out of college and go on a racial identity journey. Transracial adoptees need parents who support their racial identity development in positive ways their whole life. Let's discuss bias and racial identity for adoptees.

Bias:

Definition: Bias is disproportionate weight in favor of or against an idea or thing, usually in a way that is closed-minded, prejudicial, or unfair.

Fact: Everyone has biased views and opinions.

The first thing you have to accept when it comes to bias is that we all have them. It is impossible not to. Often these are automatic assumptions we have developed over time. Let's say you get cut off by a Hispanic driver and now, to you, all Hispanic drivers are bad drivers. A more realistic way this may play out in society is if a Hispanic driver cuts you off and then at your job as a loan officer, you don't give auto loans to Hispanic people unless they meet an unrealistic set of criteria.

Bias creeps into our lives in many more ways than you may realize. Here are the two main ways:

Explicit Bias: Explicit bias is the attitudes and beliefs we have about a person or group on a conscious level. Much of the time, these biases and their expression arise as the direct result of a perceived threat.

Implicit Bias: Implicit biases are unconscious attitudes and stereotypes that can manifest in our lives.

Most of us are in tune with our explicit biases. These aren't always negative either. You don't like spicy curry not because you don't like Indian people or food, but just because spicy food is not something you enjoy. You have a strong preference for sweet and savory food and that's great. What would be a negative explicit bias is if you hate Indian people for X reason so you refuse to eat Indian food or go to their restaurants.

Implicit bias is a little more complicated. These are biases that are formed by our surroundings and the kind of media we consume. If you don't grow up around Black people or have them in your community, but you're watching shows and movies that consistently portray Black characters in criminal roles, then subconsciously your viewpoint is being shaped. I know because this is my story.

I grew up in a home where no one said explicitly negative things about Black people. No one told me to be scared of Black people or that all Black people were "hood", but those views were ingrained in me. I remember the first time I went to Morehouse homecoming with a friend of mine, we came across a chess competition, and for some reason, I was shocked to see Black people playing chess - I had only ever seen white people play chess. I remember having to unlearn so many biases I didn't realize I had until I was living in an all-Black community. I had to deal with the fact I was extremely uncomfortable around people that looked just like me for reasons that had no merit.

This is why having a diverse community is so important. Media plays tricks on us and shows us more of what we already believe, not reality. When we experience community with people that don't look or sound like us, we realize the assumptions we made in our heads about that group of people. The best way to confront your biases is to work to be hyper-conscious of them. If you notice a weird or uncomfortable feeling when walking past someone of a different race and can't figure out why, maybe it has been unconsciously ingrained into you without you knowing.

Why is this important?

There are millions of benefits to growing in your awareness of your biases. You will likely build deeper and better relationships with people that aren't exactly like you and you will be much more kind and empathic in general to all people. **The main reason bias is important to understand as a transracial parent is that when you become aware of your biases you will also understand how the world will see your child.** The feelings you have around and about people that look like your child are the same feelings other people will have around your child. Your child will become aware of these feelings as well. If you are always clutching your purse when walking past people that look like them or crossing the street, they will notice and likely copy. The problem is that they can't escape their existence as a person of color. **Your child will be treated by the world the same way you and your community treat people that look like them.**

RACIAL IDENTITY FOR ADOPTEES

*R*acial identity is a complex and multifaceted aspect of an adoptees identity. It encompasses not only the physical characteristics that are associated with a particular race but also the cultural, historical, and social factors that shape a person's experiences and worldview.

For adoptees and foster children, racial identity can be especially challenging to navigate. They may not have grown up in communities that reflected their racial background or may have experienced discrimination or prejudice that has impacted their sense of self.

You must be intentional in your efforts, as an adoptive parent, to create an environment that supports and celebrates their child's racial identity.

One way to do this is by acknowledging and talking openly about race and racism. This means being honest about the experiences that your child may face as a

21

person of color and providing them with the tools and resources they need to navigate these challenges. It also means being willing to listen to their experiences and concerns without judgment and creating a safe space for them to express their thoughts and feelings.

Another important step is to seek out and participate in diverse communities and activities. This can include attending cultural festivals, participating in community organizations, or enrolling your child in activities that celebrate their heritage. By doing so, you expose your child to a range of perspectives and experiences and help them feel more connected to their racial identity.

It's also important to provide your child with positive role models and mentors who share their racial background. This can help your child develop a sense of pride and belonging in their identity and provide them with a sense of community and support.

Helping your child develop a positive racial identity is an ongoing process that requires patience, understanding, and a willingness to learn and grow. By creating an environment that supports and celebrates your child's racial identity, you can help them navigate the complexities of their identity with confidence and pride.

Adoptees like myself who did not grow up in communities with people that looked like us have struggled immensely with racial identity. Struggling between the reality of being a person of color, but never feeling fully accepted or seen as such. This is why racial mirrors are the best thing you can do for your child. It is hard for us to see ourselves in communities with people that look like us if we never saw people that looked like us growing up.

To start helping your child develop a positive racial identity, you have to acknowledge race. Being color blind is ignoring the unique experience your child is having and what other people of color have. You can not take a color-blind approach to transracial parenting and expect your child to ever trust you with their experiences as a person of color. In the United States race means something about you whether you like it or not.

Adoptees have to deal with being a person of color in America whether you believe in racism or not. As we saw in the summer of 2020 with George Floyd, racism is still alive and could affect your child. By acknowledging race and racism you not only show your child you see them but you also create trust with them, assuring them they can come to you if something ever happens.

Even if you do everything "right" your child may still struggle with their racial identity as an adult. What you can do is always direct them to the racial mirrors you put in their life and remind them they are loved. All of us adoptees and foster children experience this journey differently, but if you follow the steps in the next chapter, you are at least setting them up for success and giving them a great foundation to find confidence in themself.

STEP BY STEP

Ages: 0 - 5

Main Objective: *You are trying to help your child develop positive thoughts and feelings about their race as they slowly start to notice they look different.*

At this stage, your child doesn't need lectures about race or racism. What they need is to be surrounded by love and positivity in all aspects. You can start helping them develop positive associations with themselves by having toys, books, TV shows, and movies that all have characters, especially main characters, that look like them.

Ages: 5 - 12

Main Objective: *You are becoming a safe place to talk about their insecurities and any comments being made to them about being of a different race.*

It is likely your adoptee is starting to notice more and more that they are different from you and different from many of the families in your circles and school. This is where you start to establish yourself as the safe space to talk about these insecurities and race. Ask questions about what is going on at school or how they feel at school, church, etc.

Chances are other kids are making comments about your child looking different than you. Even if they are innocent comments, kids do not want to feel different; they want to fit in and be liked. You should be creating space for your kid to talk through their emotions. This is important even if they aren't angry about the comments or about being adopted. This makes it clear to your child that you will make space for them to feel different feelings and they don't have to feel wrong or bad for feeling insecure about looking different than you. Adoptees in general struggle with feeling wrong or bad for not being happy about being adopted all the time. The truth is that even though I love my adoptive parents and am grateful for the life I have had - I wasn't always happy about it. Adoptees, especially transracially adopted children, need you as the parent to make room for them to love you and not love the life they are experiencing. The more room you make for them to process comments made and their insecurity with you the more trust you will build with them and that trust is necessary as you start having more difficult conversations about race in their teen years.

This is a great time to start going to a barbershop/salon. You should also be making a big effort to find racial mirrors for your child which may mean changing your community. I have heard great stories of families finding African dance lessons to help their children see more people that look like themselves.

Here are some cultural events and resources that you can explore with your children:

1. Lunar New Year Festivals - Lunar New Year is celebrated by many Asian cultures, including Chinese, Vietnamese, and Korean. Many cities throughout the United States host Lunar New Year festivals, which can include dragon dances, lion dances, fireworks, traditional

music and food, and other cultural activities. Some examples of cities that host Lunar New Year festivals include:

- San Francisco, California

- New York City, New York

- Houston, Texas

- Seattle, Washington

- Los Angeles, California

2. African American Cultural Festivals - African American cultural festivals are held throughout the United States and showcase a wide range of cultural activities, including music, dance, art, and food. Some examples of African American cultural festivals include:

- AfroPunk Festival - Brooklyn, New York

- Essence Festival - New Orleans, Louisiana

- Juneteenth Festival - various cities throughout the United States

- National Black Arts Festival - Atlanta, Georgia

3. Native American Pow Wows - Pow wows are events that celebrate Native American culture and include traditional dances, music, and food. Many cities throughout the United States host pow wows, and some of the largest include:

- Gathering of Nations Pow Wow - Albuquerque, New Mexico

- Denver March Pow Wow - Denver, Colorado

- Red Earth Pow Wow - Oklahoma City, Oklahoma

- Stanford Pow Wow - Stanford, California

4. Museums and Cultural Centers - Museums and cultural centers offer a wealth of resources for adoptive parents and their children to learn about different cultures and histories. Some examples include:

- Smithsonian National Museum of African American History and Culture - Washington, D.C.

- National Museum of the American Indian - New York City, New York and Washington, D.C.

- Japanese American National Museum - Los Angeles, California

- National Museum of Mexican Art - Chicago, Illinois

5. Community Events - Many communities host events and celebrations that showcase their cultural traditions and history. Some examples include:

- Chinese New Year Parade - San Francisco, California

- Dia de los Muertos - various cities throughout the United States

- Kwanzaa Celebrations - various cities throughout the United States

- Holi Festival of Colors - various cities throughout the United States

These are just a few examples of the many cultural events and resources available to you and your children.

By participating in these activities and exploring your childs cultural heritage together, you can help your children develop a positive racial identity and create connections to their cultural background.

Ages: 13 - 18

Main Objective: *You are preparing your child for how the world will see and treat them.*

At this point, it is time to have hard conversations about race and racism. We want to gradually let our children know about the dangers and privileges they don't have as people of color that their white friends may have. If you have put yourself in a community with people that look like your child, other parents in your circle will be having similar conversations with their children.

There are countless stories of transracial adoptees having the police called on them for just living. There was a popular news story a few years ago of a Black adoptee being arrested for being in his own home because the neighbors had only ever seen his white parents and called the police when they saw a Black man inside the house. These are the moments your child, sadly, needs to be prepared for.

Article: https://www.huffpost.com/entry/black-teen-mistaken-burglar_n_5954138

How to Behave in Public

At this point in your child's life, you will not always be with them. When they are out with their friends they need to understand how to behave for their own safety. Your child, especially if they are male identifying/presenting, needs to know to not play with fake guns in public. No one should be doing this, but even considering nerf, BB, or airsoft guns is important. We can not control other people's ignorance or blatant racism. Your job is to protect your child first, just like Black families do. You need to make sure your child understands how the world may see them.

How to Talk to Police

Adopted children of color need to be prepared for issues while driving even if they never end up happening. We have all seen the countless videos of people of color getting pulled over and it going wrong.

After I moved back from Atlanta my mom was extremely worried about driving. She used to ask that I keep my license and insurance on the dashboard while I drive because she read about Black mothers having their sons do that. I think this is great advice especially as they are just starting to drive and driving in unfamiliar areas. I would add that a dashboard camera never hurts either. This could come in handy if and when accidents happen.

When getting pulled over your child should be as respectful and compliant as they can be. If an officer is being disrespectful and evidently racist, the time to handle it is after the interaction. Though extremely sad and wrong, people of color are often seen as not compiling when they ask questions or resist in any way. The most important thing is your child making it home.

Age: 18+

Main Objective: *You are being open and supportive as they start to process and understand their story and the world.*

At this point, you have established yourself as a safe space and have had hard conversations about race and the racism your child may experience. Your job now is to support and listen. It is likely your adoptee will experience racism and be more emotionally connected to events that happen. You should be there to listen and support when those things happen.

Your child will also probably start to process and understand their adoption/foster care experience. This can lead to a lot of emotional unrest for many adoptees. They may bring up areas in which they did not feel seen by you or the community you raised them in. They may pursue birth family reunification or a birth country trip. Though I understand the insecurity this brings parents, you must work hard to understand your child is trying to put together pieces of who they are and where they come from that. These are questions you cannot answer for them. Adoptees and foster children can experience information poverty in which they have so little information about where they come from or why they are the way they are that they begin to feel distraught. This is not because they don't love you. It's that despite the great upbringing they had they still have to live as adoptees/foster alum. They still have to face the fact that they didn't grow up with their birth family. Feelings of abandonment may come to the forefront especially as they try to develop their own relationships as adults.

They are going to need you to be patient and to understand that this new journey for them is not about you. If you make it about you, that is when adoptees feel they have to put up walls and hide from you. Respect that your child is an adult and that they still have a lot to learn and grow through.

Q&A

What do I do if I don't live in a diverse area?

*L*iving in an area with little diversity can certainly present challenges when it comes to supporting your child's racial identity development. However, there are still steps you can take to ensure that your child feels seen, heard, and valued for who they are.

One option is to look for nearby cities or towns with more diverse populations. This could include areas with larger Black, Hispanic, Asian, or Indigenous communities. Research local cultural festivals, events, and organizations such as the NAACP or Be the Bridge chapters. You can plan day trips to these places and participate in events that celebrate diversity and different cultures. This will expose your child to a wider range of people and experiences, and provide opportunities for them to feel connected to their racial identity.

Another idea is to seek out diversity in your child's media consumption. Look for books, TV shows, movies, and other media that features diverse characters and perspectives. This can help your child see themselves reflected in the media they consume and can also help them develop empathy and understanding for people from different backgrounds.

Additionally, you can seek out resources and training on anti-racism and experiences of adoptees. There are many organizations and individuals who offer workshops, webinars, and other resources on topics such as anti-racism, cultural competency, and adoptee experiences, like Identity. By educating yourself and your family on these topics, you can better support your child's racial and cultural identity development.

Finally, it's important to remember that you don't have to do this alone. Seek out support from other parents who are also raising children from diverse backgrounds. Joining support groups, either in-person or online, can provide a sense of community and a place to share experiences and resources. You can also seek out the guidance of professionals, such as therapists or adoption counselors, who can provide support and guidance as you navigate the unique challenges of raising a child from a different racial or cultural background.

What do I do if my family doesn't believe in racism?

The first step is to have an open and honest conversation with your family members. Try to understand why they have these beliefs and express your concerns about how it could affect your child. It's important to be clear about what behaviors are unacceptable and how they make you feel. Be firm but respectful in your communication, and try to find common ground where possible.

If your family members continue to make inappropriate comments or refuse to acknowledge the existence of racism, it may be necessary to limit or even cut off contact with them. While this can be a difficult decision, it's essential to prioritize your child's well-being and protect them from harmful influences. Consider seeking support from other family members or friends who share your values and can provide a positive environment for your child.

It's also important to continue educating yourself and your child about racism and its effects. Seek out resources, attend workshops or events, and engage in conversations with other parents or experts in the field. By staying informed and advocating for your child, you can create a supportive and inclusive environment that celebrates diversity and empowers your child to thrive.

What do I do when a stranger makes inappropriate comments about my child/adoption?

Adoptive and foster parents commonly have uncomfortable experiences with strangers. In these encounters and while receiving random questions from strangers, remember that your story is your story and your child's story is theirs. You do not owe anyone any information about how that child ended up in your home or their life before being adopted or in care.

It can be helpful to prepare some responses ahead of time for when these situations arise. This can help you feel more confident and in control in the moment. For example, you could respond to inappropriate comments by saying something like, "Actually, our family's story is personal and private. We don't discuss it with strangers." or "I appreciate your interest, but that's not something I'm comfortable talking about, its my childs story."

It's also important to prioritize your child's feelings and well-being in these situations. Depending on the age and personality of your child, they may feel embarrassed or uncomfortable when strangers ask personal questions about their adoption. Be sure to check in with your child afterwards and offer them comfort and support. Let them know that it's okay to set boundaries and that you're proud of them for standing up for themselves and their story.

What do I do if my child isn't interested in doing cultural activities/events or talking about race?

It's important to remember that every child is unique and has their own interests and preferences. While it's important to expose your child to their cultural heritage and race, it's also important to respect their wishes if they are not interested in participating in cultural activities or discussing race at the moment.

However, you can still create opportunities for your child to learn about their culture and race in a fun and engaging way. You can try incorporating cultural foods into your family meals, playing music from their culture, or watching movies or reading books featuring characters that look like your child. You can also plan family trips to cultural festivals or museums to expose your child to different cultural experiences.

It's important to have open and honest communication with your child about why learning about their culture and race is important, but also respecting their boundaries and allowing them to take the lead in their own learning journey.

Remember that cultural and racial identity is a journey that evolves over time, and your child may become more interested in learning about their culture and race as they grow older. The key is to create a safe and supportive environment where your child feels comfortable exploring their identity at their own pace.

Got more questions? Join the Identity Learning Community!

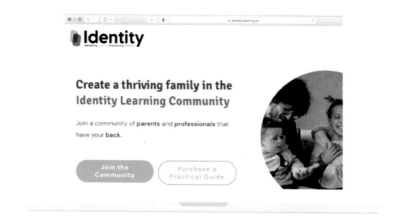

JOIN THE THRIVE COMMUNITY

was this guide helpful?

This guide and all our up coming guides,

webinars, support groups, and content are

free for Learning Community members!

JOIN TODAY

IDENTITYLEARNING.CO

WHEN PARENTS
ARE EQUIPPED

CHILDREN ARE
EMPOWERED

AND WHEN
CHILDREN ARE
EMPOWERED

FAMILIES THRIVE

JOIN TODAY

IDENTITYLEARNING.CO